Westbound and Down

Series #1

Bad Blood

DANNY HARWELL

America Star Books

Softcover 9781630845445
PUBLISHED BY AMERICA STAR BOOKS, LLLP
www.americastarbooks.com

Printed in the United States of America

Chapter One

It was about 7:30 in the morning when I resumed my duties as a newly promoted, fully fledged engineer for the Amtrak/ New York & Atlantic Railway "Atlantic Coast" route, extending from Washington, District of Columbia to the aspiring port city of Jacksonville, Florida. My former "Brother in Arms", Noah was now gone, running the daily freights from Richmond on an entirely different portion of the line. I had already begun to miss him, remembering the last time we spoke at Christmas time after being promoted and defeating one of the most lethal threats to our railroad infrastructure. It was already around my estimated arrival time of 8:10 when I got to the station. I hurried inside to the train crew office and punched in. My two good friends, Jubei and Shadow were waiting upon my fairly timely arrival. Shadow was going to be working alongside me as my new student engineer on today's #97 Silver Meteor headed for Miami. Jubei smiled. "Well, well." She beamed. "Look who's bright and early this fine spring morning." "Well, you know what they say…" I replied. "The early wolf catches the deer" They each shared a laugh and I sat down and began discussing today's work order with Shadow. Not even a minute after our discussion had ended, the crew lounge door opened to reveal a stark grey coyote dressed in a beige Polyester jacket, blue jeans, and a pair of desert brown Timberland brand boots. A sea of eyes in the room including my own, were now focused on him. He thoroughly scoped out the room before he spoke. "Is Jubei Stahlson around?" Jubei was just about to silently raise her hand before I stood up and came face to face with the coyote. "Who wants to know?" I said in an icy tone. "Devin Regis, sir. I am going to be working with Jubei Stahlson as their new trainee. Now, I'd appreciate if you could please point them out." He replied, seemingly unphased by my bitterness. I simply said nothing, in fear of ruining my good reputation with Mr. Jackson and the rest of the railroad and instead just glared at the coyote before motioning for Jubei to come forth and saying to her "Keep an eye on this one. He's nothing but bad blood for all of us." The coyote suddenly looked hurt by my remark as I stormed out with Shadow to the station platforms.

Chapter Two

I was glad when our train was finally ready on platform 8 at 9:20. We would be working the southbound palmetto today with seeming all nonstop service from D.C. to Savannah, Georgia. The power for today's train happened to be a usual, fairly new SD70ACE; number 3046 to be exact, but with our lead unit being ex CSX GP15-1 number 1550; the oldest locomotive remaining on the Amtrak/NY&A roster, which normally hung around the station performing hostling duties or making up long distance trains in Ivy City Yard. We climbed aboard into 1550's small-but spacious spartan cab and waited for all of the nearly 50 to 95 passengers to embark. We were ready to leave at 9:30. Slowly easing off the train brake as usual, I click the throttle back a few notches and turn on the bell as we inch slowly under the station. We had been going pretty well for the most part. The rails gave a rhythmical hum and signal lights shown green in the morning light as we passed, by now getting up to the track speed of around 60 miles an hour. By the time we reached the Virginia/North Carolina state line though, our speed began to suddenly decline rapidly until we could eventually do no more than a crawl of 19 to 20 miles an hour. I immediately got on the horn with dispatch who diverted us into the siding at Wilson, just 20 miles east of Rocky Mount. After a full inspection, we soon came to realize that the slip control mechanism of our lead unit had failed, resulting in intense wheel slip and our two units being dragged down by the weight of the heavy coaches. I sighed and climbed with Shadow back into the cab of our engine. It was going to be a very long wait.

Chapter Three

Waiting. That's just what we had been doing for nearly 3 hours straight. Fortunately, having an open and jovial assistant engineer like Shadow to chat with was enough to occupy me. But even he was starting to get a little on edge, having to stare out at the same patch of brush and trees beside the tracks. Just when we felt like abandoning all hope, we hear the sounding of a horn in the distance, for the Lance road crossing. A minute later, two freight locomotives, SD70MAC number 7751 and ES44AC number 448, slowly roll up on the mainline and stop just outside the conductor's side window. I scowled at the coyote Shadow had leaned out the window to converse with, as I realized he was the same coyote I had confronted before at the yards. "Looks like you two got yourselves in a bit of a jam, eh? Don't worry. Jubei and I volunteered to help you guys as soon as we got the call." Suddenly, the flame burning inside of me began to die down. No coyote ever volunteered to help out a wolf or any other animal for anything, even if it was just out of the kindness of their heart. Something about him was different. Without wasting another minute of time, Jubei and the coyote moved their power forward, over the siding switch and were soon coupled in front of our lead unit. Jubei radioed to us from her place in the conductor's seat. "You boys ready?" "As ready as we'll ever be" I responded eagerly. The coyote gave two taps on 7751's stellar K5LA horn for the "forward" signal and we gently pull out onto the mainline. We reach the Florence, South Carolina station at 4:15 PM, just as our 12 hours on duty had come to an end. After some weary passengers had given their thanks to Jubei and her companion for the rescue, I approached the coyote and began to give my own gratitude to him for the selfless act. "Devin?" I asked. He gave me a funny look, suggesting he was still a little offended by my sour remark earlier. I continued to speak. "I was wrong. You're really not such a bad guy after all. It's just I came from a job where the motto was 'trust no one'. I really didn't mean any harm by what

I said back in DC. I just hope that you can find it somewhere in your heart to forgive me?" Devin let the words soak in for a moment then he smiled and said. "Think nothing of it, Aaron. I know what it feels like to be bullied by members of the opposite race. But I've learned to just put the past behind me and move on, ya know. Let by gones be by gones, live and let be." He put his thumb up and flashed me a warm smile. "Friends?" He asked kindly. "Friends." I replied, flashing a similar smile and returning the thumbs up. Just then, the conductor gave his signal and Devin thought he and Jubei had better go. I waved a quick goodbye to Devin as he gave the two warning toots on the horn and throttled up for the rest of the journey to Savannah, Georgia. As for Shadow and I, it was time to retire to the nearby Hilton Garden Inn for a good days rest.

DarkFang

Chapter One

Sundown, Saturday evening. The date is the first of July. A very special month for me and the rest of my longtime family of workmates over at the Amtrak/ New York & Atlantic Railway. It was the day of my birth and Mr. Jackson had decided to let a few of us take some well needed time off in recognition of it. To celebrate, the 4 of us had all headed over to Hutch's new place on Pennsylvania Avenue, not far from the station. We sat idly at the kitchen table, drinks in our paws and glasses in the air in preparation for a toast.

"To the Rogue Warriors, the best of friends, and best of all, the glorious defeat of the two vicious criminal scum, Danny Miller and Zeke Cortez. With the defeat of Cortez, by our one and only Norman Hutch." There was a chorus of cheers and joy filled shouts as we clung our glasses together and everyone wished me a happy 26th. Everyone had an unremarkable sense of joy and relief, as seen on their warm, smiling faces. Everyone except Hutch, who wore an expression plagued with the woeful feelings of worry and dread. "Something wrong, man?" I asked him in my usual friendly tone. He made a "follow me" gesture with his paw and I walked close behind him down into the basement. He stopped somewhere beyond the bottom of the stairs, in an isolated room with only an old timey big screen TV and an old, worn out couch for company. I gave him a look of concern and asked. "Hutch, what the hell is wrong with you? You act like you've just seen a ghost." He inhaled and drew out a long, nervous sigh before speaking. "Remember when I said that Cortez would never be a problem for us again, back at the Christmas party?" I nodded. "Yeah...?" "Well, turns out I was wrong." "What?" I said mortified. "He's alive and on his way back to the U.S. as we speak." Hutch replied, panicking. He began to pace the floor anxiously. "Why are you just now coming to me with this?" I asked, now horrified. "I'm sorry, Aaron. I knew I should have told you before. But I just didn't want you to worry. Anyway, it's out of our hands now-..." Suddenly, I grabbed the neck of Hutch's shirt with both paws and slammed his body against the nearby wall. A voice I did not recognize escaped my mouth. "No. It is in your hands. You will bring me that scumbag's head on a silver platter or you. Will. Die." Hutch stared at me in utter shock and disbelief. I couldn't believe I would ever say something like that to one of my dearest friends who would be with me until the end. I didn't believe it. Something about me was just horribly wrong. "I... I need to go." I said in my normal voice and raced up the stairs as quickly as I could. I stepped into my boots at the door and grabbed the keys to my car, not even bothering to bid my farewells to the other party guests.

Chapter Two

I sat alone on the bed in my room, feelings of melancholy and self directed anger slowly starting to devour me alive. With Ashley working the late shift at her workplace, and Lilly on call at the hospital, I was glad to come home to an empty house and have some solitude. I picked up a framed picture of me and the lioness I once knew and loved, staring at it with a pained expression on my face and letting out a long and heavy sigh. Just then, the voice I didn't recognize spoke again. "Well, well. Finally reached your breaking point eh, Aaron?" "What's going on? Who the hell are you?" I asked nervously. "Don't worry. I can help get you what you so desperately desire. Sweet revenge for your fallen lover. Isn't that what you want?" "Yes." I answered after a brief pause. "Then you must trust me." "You still haven't told me a thing about who you are." The voice chuckled darkly. "Look in the mirror, and you will soon see the truth." I stood up and made my way to the bathroom across the room. I turned on the light and my eyes widened in surprise. There, in the mirror, was the most grotesque reflection of myself I had ever seen. My fur was now all black, similar to Shadow's, with red markings around the left side of my face and body. My eyes were serpentine and glowed a goldish yellow color. In my agape mouth, were rows of needle sharp teeth, slightly longer and sharper than normal wolf teeth. The voice spoke up again. "You see, I live in you. And together, we can avenge your previous mate's death and take our vengence on the killer himself. The only question is: Are you in?" "Oh yeah." I replied with little to no hesitation. "I'm in."

Chapter Three

I lay quietly on the sectional in my living room, saying "damn" to myself as I tried desperately to fall into the comforting arms of sleep. Aaron was my best friend, my faithful companion. What the hell kind of wolf was I to ever let him down. Before I could even think about closing my eyes, there were four knocks at the front door. I placed my bare feet on the hard wood floor and gradually made my way over to answer it. When I was nearly 3 feet from it, the door suddenly burst open and there stood an all black wolf with red markings on the left side of his sinister looking face. He was clad in a black leather trenchcoat, black khaki pants, and a pair of long, black biker type boots. I stared deep into his gold serpentine eyes and glanced at his menacing grin which revealed a set of razor sharp teeth. "Norman Hutch" He said in a chilling voice. "It's time to answer for your lies." I thrust out my tightly clenched fist, in an attempt to get him with a cheap shot to his jaw. With lightning fast reflexes, he blocked the punch with the palm of his paw and returned with a punch of his own which sent me flying half way across the living room and landing hard on the wood floor. I shook it off and attempted to stand, only to receive another right hook straight to my muzzle. I turned my head and spit a bit of blood on the floor before he grabbed me by the throat and hauled me up 6 inches off the floor. "Who the hell are you?" I asked him, just barely choking out the words. "What do you want from me?" "That is nowhere near important. What I want is information on a certain someone named Zeke Cortez. And I believe you two have already met." "I'm not telling you a goddamn thing." I snarled. He growled and tightened his grip around my neck. "Speak! Now" "Or what?" I deadpanned. He then drew a silver Colt 1911, very similar to the one Aaron always carries and placed the end of it against my temple. "Or I will officially end you right here, right now." "Alright. Alright!" I answered, now in fear of my life. "Look. If you're wondering where he is, he's probably half way across the border, on his way from Argentina by now. That's all I know. I swear to god." "Good boy." He said giving me a light pat on the head. "Now, was that really so difficult?" He released his grip and dropped me to the floor, sputtering and gasping for air, trying desperately to catch my breath. He turned to leave but I grabbed his leg and said wearily. "You still haven't told me who you are." "I'm DarkFang." He replied and landed one final punch right to my temple. The world went dark.

Chapter Four

11:05 AM, the next morning. Shadow and I were just pulling into Union Station, having been on a short commuter run from Washington to Baltimore and had now just made the return trip back to DC. I gently coaxed our train into the station and stopped at platform B-3. After all of the passengers disembark, Shadow opens the assistant engineer's side door on GP39H-2 number 74 and we step out onto the platform, enroute to the crew office to sign out. We reached the double doors and made our way inside, heading toward the back of the station to the crew quarters. We had just reached the door when Shadow suddenly shouted "Look out!" He yanked me down to the floor, just as a bullet whizzed by my left ear and embedded itself into the wood of the door. I turned around to be greeted by my number one target. There, alongside two Ocelot bodyguards, stood Zeke Cortez. A look of surprise was present on his face and he pointed his finger in a way of saying "You again?". He gestured to one of the guards who now raised his M14 rifle and prepared to fire on us again. We simultaneously drew our weapons and took cover behind two nearby columns as another shot rang out through the air. I poked my head out just in time to see Cortez dipping it toward the main hall of the station. "Alright. Lets ice these pricks." I said to Shadow. "I'll go one way, you go the other." "Roger that" He saluted and fired two shots at the Ocelot guards, both bullets hitting their target. When no one was looking, My fur began to go all black, my teeth grew sharper, and I once again let DarkFang begin to take total control of my mind and body. I approached the other two guards and spoke in that bone chilling voice. "Ok, assholes. You wanna dance? Let's dance." I stepped forth just as the guard raised his M14. After sending an elbow to his face, I snatched the M14 from his open paws and cracked him across the head with the buttstock, knocking him out cold. With precision aiming, I raised the M14 and fired one shot, hitting the other guard in the throat. He sputtered and gurgled on his own blood before collapsing to the floor. When I was sure he was incapacitated, I slung the strap of the rifle over my shoulder and grabbed a machete and sheath off the body of the other Ocelot. I ran past hoards of screaming animals as I bounced back, hot on Cortez's trail. I rounded the corner to find the two separate doors of the station bathrooms. Pistol drawn, I burst through the door to find Cortez with his back pressed up against the wall looking terrified. He pointed a finger and said, breathily. "You... You're not that cop." I chuckled menacingly, smirking. "No. I'm not. Not anymore." I holstered my Colt and approached him, slowly. I decided it was time to have a little fun with the hunter before he became the hunted. He stepped up from the wall and got into a fighting stance, only to be hammered by a right hook to his muzzle. He thrust out his fist, only to swing at air as

I quickly ducked under his left hook. I grabbed his arm in mid punch and brought my fist down hard to hear the sickening crunch. He howled in pain and I kicked him against the wall with such a force that the tiles shattered. I approached him as he sat dazed and writhing in pain. "Please. Please don't kill me." He pleaded as I stopped 2 inches in front of him. "Yeah, you'd like that wouldn't you?" I said in a mocking tone. I drew the machete from the sheath and held it at my side. "But, you see, you don't always get what you like in life. Life has its twists and turns. I learned that the hard way, and unfortunately, looks like you'll have to do the same. Goodbye, Cortez." I thrust my paw forward; piercing the blade straight through his heart and ripping it back out. He fell forward and lay face down on the floor, in a pool of his own blood.

I unholstered my Colt and fired two shots into his head, silencing the young coyote forever.

Chapter Five: *Epilogue*

I came to and found myself slumped against the wall next to the body of the now finished Zeke Cortez. Suddenly, just as I was trying to get my bearings, the bathroom door opened and one of our railroad's police officers stepped in. It took me only a few seconds to realize that the officer was Hutch by his signature long black and grey fur. He took a minute to survey the scene before walking over to me and extending a paw, easing me onto my feet. He gave me a brotherly slap on the back and said. "You did it, brotha. You did something even I couldn't. Nice job." I smiled and then glanced at my reflection in the pristine mirror. My fur was back to its original golden red coloring and my eyes had now returned to their traditional shape and light brown color. "Welcome back, old friend." Hutch said, smiling. "You won't tell a soul about this. Will you, Hutch?" I asked, innocently. "My lips are sealed." Replied Hutch. "You can for sure count on me this time." "Thanks, man." He smiled warmly and we shook paws in a brotherly like shake. We strolled out to the station lobby and made our way out the double doors to the parking lot, ignoring the flashing lights of the emergency vehicles as we went. It was good to be pals once again.

The End

CPSIA information can be obtained at www.ICGtesting.com
Printed in the USA
BVOW01s1427070414

349965BV00001B/55/P

9 781630 845445